10 THINGS YOUR PROBATION OFFICER WON'T TELL YOU, BUT SHOULD

PJ Rios

10 THINGS YOUR PROBATION OFFICER WON'T TELL YOU, BUT SHOULD

ISBN: 979-8-89228-791-3 (Paperback)
ISBN: 979-8-89228-792-0 (eBook)

Library of Congress Control Number:

Printed in the United States of America

CONTENTS

DEDICATION

To my family: Matthew, Tara, Tyler and Patrick, without whom, I never would have the strength to complete and publish this book.

PROLOGUE

Probation is never easy. It involves allowing a stranger into your life—someone who will scrutinize your every move and, if necessary, can restrict your freedom. The reality of probation can feel invasive and restrictive, whether you are a juvenile or an adult. When a judge places you under a probation officer's (PO) supervision, a new chapter begins—one characterized by strict rules that challenge your sense of independence. Suddenly, you're bound by a curfew, prohibited from consuming alcohol, forced to end certain relationships, and required to attend counseling sessions. Planning a vacation? Forget it—permission is mandatory. Weekly check-ins with your officer will add another layer of scrutiny, as you must explain your activities.

Be prepared for the reality of constant oversight. Your probation officer's judgments can often feel harsh, lacking the kindness you might mistakenly expect during such a vulnerable time. It's essential to toughen up and let go of any negative attitude; resistance will only tighten the restrictions on your freedom. Many enter the probation system with the mindset to manipulate, believing they can charm or deceive their way to leniency. However, these manipulative individuals often meet a well-trained officer who can see through their façade. Probation officers have years of training that allow them to read body language and detect lies, making it unwise to underestimate their ability to discern your true motives.

While probation is undeniably uncomfortable, it can also serve as a pathway to growth and self-discovery. Many individuals find that, upon completion, they have developed healthier habits and a newfound sense of clarity. This book aims to shed light on ten crucial topics that probation officers may not discuss openly but should. Whether you are currently on probation, anticipating it, or reflecting on what comes next, understanding these insights can empower you to navigate the system more effectively. Embrace this opportunity; your journey through probation can lead to a brighter, more resilient future.

CHAPTER 1

GET YOUR OWN ATTORNEY

For most people, going to court is a terrifying experience. It is where life-changing decisions are mandated, often resulting in tears shed. Some individuals leave the courtroom crying tears of immense joy, while others find themselves crying from anger and disappointment. Courtrooms are the setting for intense, emotionally charged events, and navigating this environment without proper legal representation can be daunting.

While having an attorney by your side is clearly beneficial, it's important to understand why a probation officer (PO) might not explicitly encourage you to seek one. This hesitation can arise from various factors, including the dynamics of the courtroom, the relationship between the probation officer and the attorney, and the overall goals of the probation officer in your case.

Probation officers act as intermediaries between the court and individuals on probation. Their primary responsibility is to ensure that probationers comply with the terms of their probation while advocating for rehabilitation. However, when it comes to court appearances, the dynamics shift. Courtroom participants—such as Assistant District attorneys, probation officers, and even some public defenders—often want to complete the proceedings with minimal argument. This can create lead to situations where a probation officer may not actively encourage you to hire an attorney, complicating their role in the courtroom.

There is no doubt that you are better off with a skilled attorney by your side. It is always wise to have someone knowledgeable and willing to fight for you, especially when facing probation or prison. A private attorney can provide invaluable support, particularly in cases where probation or incarceration are options due to the severity of the crime. If you cannot afford an attorney, one will be provided for you; however, you may need to prove your financial inability. Often, those provided for you are not necessarily on top of their game. While some public defenders are among the best attorneys, many lack a sense of commitment to their clients unless they are compensated directly.

Having an attorney who is willing to argue on your behalf and present you positively is the best option available. Whether you are in court for a probation violation or a sentencing hearing, if your attorney can reduce your sentence by just one year, that means one year less in prison or on probation. Investing in an attorney can be well worth for one year or more of your freedom.

From the probation officer's perspective, recommending that you hire an attorney could complicate their role in court. If they recommend to the judge and you have your own attorney present, the attorney's voice may be more highly regarded than that of the probation officer or the individual who committed the offense. This dynamic could lead to the probation officer feeling that their authority is undermined, making them less likely to encourage you to seek legal representation.

Moreover, probation officers must balance the interests of the court with the needs of the probationer. They may worry that hiring an independent attorney could complicate this balance, leading to a more adversarial relationship in court. This does not mean that probation officers do not want what is best for their clients; rather, they may feel that your own attorney could hinder their ability to effectively advocate on your behalf.

If you plan to hire an attorney, it's crucial to find someone who is not only knowledgeable but also empathetic to your situation. After a crime has been committed, your future depends on your defense. You can never spend too much on a good attorney. Your attorney should be motivated to help you, possess strong negotiating skills, and communicate effectively with both the judge and you. If your initial meeting with an attorney does not go well, it is wise to seek representation from someone else. Any uneasy feeling during that meeting should serve as a warning sign to look for another attorney.

On court day, it's essential for your attorney to not only understand your story but also present it with compassion. Attorneys are trained in law and know how to navigate the legal system. Their education and analytical skills should be evident in court. They can handle most of the questions for you and provide answers that highlight your positive qualities. Each question is an opportunity for the attorney to showcase your strengths and help diminish the negative perception of the crime you committed.

The emotional weight of going to court cannot be overstated. Having an advocate standing by your side during such a terrifying time is invaluable. An attorney can act like a protective shield, bravely stepping forward to face the challenges ahead. Hiring an attorney can significantly increase your chances of a favorable outcome in your case and provides peace of mind knowing that you have a skilled professional on your side.

While a probation officer may not explicitly encourage you to hire an attorney, it is crucial to understand that doing so is in your best interest. The complexities of the legal system can be overwhelming, and having someone familiar with court rules and procedures can greatly influence the outcome of your case.

In conclusion, even if a probation officer does not actively suggest hiring an attorney, recognizing the importance of legal representation in court is vital. The dynamics of the courtroom, the role of the probation officer, and the emotional weight of the situation all contribute to this complex environment. Ultimately, having an attorney by your side gives you the best chance of achieving a favorable outcome, ensuring your rights are protected and your story is told compassionately. Remember, an attorney can provide legal advice; this book cannot. Therefore, when facing the daunting experience of court, prioritize hiring a skilled attorney who can effectively advocate for you. Your future may depend on it.

CHAPTER 2

PAPER TELLS YOUR STORY

In the beginning, the offender is seen by the justice system as merely a story on paper. No one has met the offender except for the police officer involved at the scene, who wrote the report detailing the incident. This police report serves as the first introduction of the offender to the judge, probation officer, and district attorney. For many individuals, the day of the incident is one they regret and wish to put behind them as soon as possible. Unfortunately, the crimes committed are outlined in the police report, describing the details of the offense in a way that can be difficult to confront.

The severity of the offense, along with the specifics described by the police officer in their report, plays a critical role in determining the offender's sentencing. Ideally, the offender would have respected the police, and the report would reflect that. Regardless of the offender's actions, these will be documented, and that documentation will ultimately influence the level of consequences they face. In this context, how the offender is perceived on paper often matters more than how they appear in the courtroom. While it is advisable for offenders to present themselves well on the day of sentencing and use polite language when addressing the judge, the reality is that the crimes and typical sentencing for those offenses will heavily influence the judge's decision.

The importance of the offender's statement on the day of the incident is significant, especially if they are innocent. Many individuals make the mistake of refusing to provide a statement when the police officer asks them to. However, if you want your side of the story heard by the judge, it is crucial to fill out a statement. This document, along with the statements from others involved in the incident, will be presented to the judge, district attorney, and probation officer. These papers together form the narrative of the case.

Deciding whether or not to write a statement can be a dilemma. The question of whether a person who has committed a crime should share their side of the story varies for each offender and their specific circumstances.

When it comes time for court, it is likely that you will not be asked to describe the incident or your role in it. Those who completed a statement at the scene have will have their story read, while those who did not risk having their narrative overlooked. This can be particularly detrimental if you believe your perspective could mitigate the consequences of your actions. However, it is essential to weigh the potential benefits of providing a statement against the risks.

While there are advantages to writing a statement, there are also significant risks, especially for those who may be guilty or whose actions could be viewed as incriminating. If you are concerned about self-incrimination, it may be advisable to refrain from completing a statement. Most attorneys would recommend against this, given the potential legal ramifications. The legal landscape can be complex, and anything you say can be used against you in court.

In many cases, offenders may feel compelled to explain their actions in hopes of providing context for a more lenient sentence. However, this desire to share their side of the story can backfire. Statements can be scrutinized and interpreted in unforeseen ways, such as an attempt to frame a crime as a moment of poor judgment, which could be viewed as a lack of accountability and lead to harsher consequences.

It's important to note that probation officers are there to help individuals navigate the aftermath of the incident and work towards moving on. When we make mistakes in life, it is best to own up to them, apologize, and learn from the experience to avoid repeating it. Probation offers a chance for restitution and allows individuals to correct their mistakes. This process may involve writing an apology letter to the victim, facilitating the offender's ability to move on. Once probation is successfully completed, securing stable employment, achieving educational goals, and establishing a positive future become viable outcomes.

However, if you refuse to take accountability for your actions and make necessary changes, this part of your life may become significantly challenging. The probation officer's role is to aid in your rehabilitation, but they are also obligated to report to the court. If your statement contradicts the information in the police report or raises more questions, it could complicate your case and negatively affect your chances of a favorable outcome.

Most people do not intentionally break the law; reoffenders are the exception. I believe the majority of individuals who find themselves in a courtroom pleading guilty are learning a difficult lesson and are unlikely to repeat that offense. While everyone's story is different, it is the offense described that will dictate the consequences you face. An attorney can help explain the possible outcomes and will guide you on whether or not to provide a statement.

If you do not have an attorney, you can gain some understanding of the consequences you might encounter by searching online for information related to the state where you committed the offense and the specific crime (e.g., "Nevada DUI"). Many attorneys advertise their services this way, often providing free information, and some may even offer a free consultation over the phone. This initial consultation can be invaluable for helping you understand your options and the potential ramifications of your choices.

In conclusion, deciding to write a statement after committing a crime involves considerable complexities. On one hand, providing a statement can allow the offender to express their side of the story, potentially influencing the judge's perception and leading to a more favorable outcome. On the other hand, the risks of self-incrimination and misinterpretation may outweigh the benefits, especially for those who may not be entirely innocent.

Ultimately, it is essential for offenders to carefully evaluate their circumstances and consult with legal counsel before making a decision. The legal landscape is can be complicated, and having a knowledgeable advocate can significantly help in navigating the intricacies of the justice system. Whether to write a statement is a personal choice that should be made with careful consideration of the potential consequences and with the guidance of a qualified attorney. In the end, the goal should be to take accountability for one's actions while also protecting one's rights and future.

CHAPTER 3

RECOMMENDATIONS ARE THE PO'S DOING AT SENTENCING

In the criminal justice system, the role of a probation officer (PO) is pivotal, especially when it comes to making recommendations to the court regarding consequences for offenders. Although the final decision rests with the judge, the insights and evaluations provided by probation officers can significantly influence the outcome of a case. Understanding this dynamic responsibility is essential for anyone navigating the complexities of the legal system.

A probation officer supervises individuals placed on probation or community supervision as an alternative to incarceration. As part of their duties, probation officers conduct interviews, investigate the backgrounds of the individuals, monitor compliance with court-ordered conditions, and make recommendations to the court regarding the individual's progress or any noncompliance with the terms of probation. This multifaceted role enables probation officers to assess the circumstances of each case and provide informed recommendations to the judge.

In some instances, the court may order a pre-sentence investigation report (PSI), which is typically prepared by the probation officer or another designated court official. The PSI includes detailed information about the defendant's personal and criminal history, such as age, education, employment history, family background, prior criminal record, and any other relevant factors the judge may consider when determining an appropriate sentence. The report may also cover the nature of the offense, the impact on the victim and the community, and any mitigating or aggravating factors relevant to the sentencing.

The PSI is a crucial document that assists the judge in determining an appropriate sentence for a defendant who has been convicted of a crime. It is typically prepared after the conviction but before sentencing. The probation officer gathers information through interviews with the defendant, family members, and other individuals, along with a review of court records and other relevant documents. Once completed, the report is submitted to the court and provided to the defense attorney and prosecutor.

The information contained in the PSI is vital for the judge in determining an appropriate sentence. It may also be used to develop a plan for any conditions of probation or supervised release that the defendant may be required to follow as part of their sentence. The PSI serves an important tool for ensuring that sentences are tailored to the individual circumstances of the defendant, promoting rehabilitation and reducing the likelihood of future criminal behavior.

In most jurisdictions, prior to court proceedings, judges receive recommendations from the probation department regarding appropriate consequences for the offenses committed. Many crimes have penalties mandated by state statutes, meaning that while judges have some discretion, the nature of the crime often dictates the resulting consequences. For example, in Nevada, drug offenses may result in fines, fees, probation, or even incarceration, while assault charges may lead to similar penalties, including community service or counseling programs.

Judges often rely on the recommendations of probation officers, especially in cases involving probation violations. At this point, the probation officer is familiar with the offender and has a history of their compliance or noncompliance with the terms of their probation. Judges typically trust the probation officer's opinion, which can lead to more favorable outcomes for offenders if the probation officer advocates for leniency.

However, it is important to note that judges have the final say in determining sentences. While they consider the recommendations of probation officers, they also have the discretion to make decisions based on their interpretation of the law and the specific circumstances of each case. This means that although probation officers play a significant role in shaping the recommendations, the ultimate decision rests with the judge.

If you are on probation and have committed a violation, the probation officer may sometimes inform you of their recommendations prior to court. However, this information may not always be disclosed upfront and could depend on the circumstances. In some cases, probation officers might withhold their recommendations, fearing that the probationer might run or commit additional crimes before the court date.

Whatever the judge decides at the time of sentencing must be followed. If you disagree with the judge's sentence, keeping that opinion to yourself is crucial. Arguing with a judge can lead to contempt of court charges, resulting in additional penalties. Judges hold significant power, and that power must be respected.

Judges are not just arbiters of the law; they are also individuals elected or appointed to their positions based on their qualifications and the trust placed in them by the community. They face immense pressure and scrutiny, as every decision they make can be subject to criticism. Navigate the complexities of public opinion while making decisions that can profoundly impact people's lives is a significant burden.

Judges are tasked with determining appropriate sentences based on the recommendations they receive, the law, and the individual circumstances of each case. They must balance the need for justice with the potential for rehabilitation, all while considering the impact of their decisions on victims, offenders, and the community. This responsibility is not for the faint of heart; it requires a level of confidence and resilience that many people may not possess.

In conclusion, probation officers play a critical role in the criminal justice system, particularly when making recommendations to the court regarding the consequences for offenders. While the ultimate decision rests with the judge, the insights and evaluations provided by probation officers can significantly influence the outcome of a case. Understanding this dynamic is essential for anyone navigating the complexities of the legal system.

The pre-sentence investigation report (PSI) is a vital tool in this process, providing judges with comprehensive information about the defendant's background, the nature of the offense, and recommendations for sentencing. Judges often rely on the recommendations of probation officers, especially in cases involving probation violations, but they also have the authority to exercise discretion and make decisions based on their interpretation of the law.

The relationship between probation officers, judges, and offenders is complex and multifaceted. Offenders must understand the importance of compliance, conduct, and the potential consequences of their actions within the legal system. By recognizing the role of probation officers and the significance of their recommendations, individuals can better navigate the challenges they face more effectively and work toward a more positive outcome in their cases.

CHAPTER 4

THE FIRST MEETING

Facing the probation system can be an intimidating experience, especially when you arrive for your first meeting with your probation officer (PO). This initial encounter can set the tone for your entire probation period, making it essential to understand its dynamics. From the moment you walk through the door, various evaluations and assessments begin, all while you deal with feelings of anxiety and paranoia.

As you enter the probation office, the atmosphere feels charged with judgment. The officer's gaze scans you, evaluating everything from your clothing to your body language. You might feel underdressed or over-dressed; however, every detail is being noticed. Your choice of attire can communicate a lot about your background and mindset. For example, inadvertently wearing gang colors might label you as a potential gang member, while a smart-casual outfit could show that you respect the situation.

If you bring a significant other with you, their presence adds another layer of scrutiny. The officer will observe your interactions, looking for signs about your character and how you relate to those close to you. Are you respectful? Do you communicate openly? These assessments are not arbitrary; they help the officer gauge your potential for rehabilitation and how you might navigate your probation.

During the meeting, your PO will review the terms and conditions of your probation, which can feel overwhelming. As they explain the requirements—such as adhering to a curfew, attending counseling sessions, and avoiding alcohol—the officer is not just informing you; they are also sizing you up, considering what might happen if you violate these terms. Feelings of paranoia may surface, and rightly so; every sigh or fidget is noticed, and every expression of discontent carefully recorded. A raised eyebrow or a restless leg can signal unease or resistance, prompting the officer to question your commitment.

The officer's demeanor during the initial meeting often tends to be demanding. Many officers approach this first encounter with serious intent, establishing a sense of authority from the start. They want you to understand the gravity of your situation. Their role is to help you, but they must also maintain control and set clear boundaries.

Body language is crucial during this first meeting. Your posture, speech, and even your breathing can be interpreted in various ways. For instance, crossing your arms and legs might suggest that you are closed off or untrusting. Slouching can indicate disrespect, while a tense posture might signal defiance or anxiety. In contrast, maintaining open body language—such as sitting up straight and avoiding barriers like bags or purses—can convey that you are willing to engage and cooperate.

Officers are trained to read these cues, which can significantly influence their perception of you. They may also watch your reactions to specific questions, looking for signs of honesty or dishonesty. Eye rolls might indicate contempt, while excessive blinking could raise suspicion of deceit. Understanding this dynamic is crucial; the more you engage openly, the better your chances of fostering a productive relationship with your probation officer.

As the meeting progresses, your probation officer will likely ask you to recount the incident that led to your probation. This is a pivotal moment. It's essential to remember that embellishing or romanticizing your crime will not benefit you. Phrases like "I should be clean" or "Why does probation have to be so hard?" can signal to the officer that you may not be taking the process seriously.

Instead, strive for honesty and accountability. Acknowledge your mistakes without trying to shift the blame. This approach not only demonstrates maturity but also lays the groundwork for the officer to help you address underlying issues. If your offenses were drug-related, for example, they may be considering whether rehabilitation is necessary, recognizing that addiction is often a form of self-harm.

At some point, you may be asked to complete a questionnaire designed to assess your level of supervision and identify any necessary therapeutic interventions. This evaluation can be conducted either verbally or through a computerized system. Answering these questions honestly is vital; doing so opens the door to receiving the help you may need. If you are dishonest, you risk prolonging your probation or even facing incarceration.

Officers often ask similar questions in different forms to identify inconsistencies. Being transparent is in your best interest, as this assessment can lead to a tailored plan that addresses your unique challenges. Remember, the intent behind this process is not punitive; it's about helping you succeed and avoid future issues.

Making a good impression in a high-pressure situation can feel impossible, but you can take steps to ensure a positive interaction. It's essential to enter the meeting with a mindset of honesty and a willingness to take responsibility for your actions. Acknowledging your past mistakes and expressing a desire to improve is crucial. Most probation officers appreciate when clients show a genuine commitment to change.

Keep in mind that probation officers often deal with individuals who lie or manipulate situations. Therefore, they may approach new clients with a degree of cynicism. If you approach them sincerely, you might find that they are willing to help you navigate the challenges of probation.

The level of supervision you receive will depend on various factors, including the nature of your offense. Generally, jurisdictions categorize probation into low, medium, and high supervision levels. Low supervision might involve minimal check-ins and mainly focuses on ensuring you complete mandated tasks such as community service. Medium supervision requires more regular contact, including urinalysis tests and home visits. High supervision is the most stringent level, often involving ankle monitors and close monitoring for an extended period.

Understanding your level of supervision can help you navigate the probation process more effectively. Regardless of the classification, knowing that completing probation can lead to a better future should motivate you to engage constructively with your officer.

The first meeting with your probation officer can feel like a daunting initiation into a world filled with rules and scrutiny. However, by recognizing the dynamics at play and approaching the encounter with honesty and a willingness to change, you can set a positive trajectory for your probation. Understand that this process is not merely punitive; it's an opportunity for growth and rehabilitation. Embrace it, take responsibility for your actions, and don't hesitate to ask for help. With the right mindset, you can successfully navigate the challenges ahead and emerge stronger on the other side.

CHAPTER 5

WHAT A PO IS AND WHAT A PO IS NOT

Probation officers are vital in the criminal justice system, serving as the primary link between courts and individuals on probation. Their responsibilities come with complexities, encompassing elements of law enforcement, counseling, and community service. However, the public perception of probation officers is often clouded by misconceptions. To clarify the reality of a probation officer's work, it's important to define their main responsibilities and dispel misconceptions.

At its core, the role of a probation officer is to supervise individuals sentenced to probation instead of prison. This supervision is a critical component of rehabilitation. Knowing the officer assigned to you, the person setting your requirements, is in your best interest. A good probation officer will work to understand your unique circumstances, challenges, and needs. They ensure you comply with the terms of your probation, which may include attending counseling sessions, maintaining employment, and avoiding further legal trouble.

Probation officers are also officers of the court, meaning they have a significant role in the judicial process. They prepare reports for the court, make recommendations regarding sentencing, and testify in hearings. This aspect of their job highlights their authority and the trust placed in them by the judicial system. More than just enforcers, they are also advocates for rehabilitation, aiming to help individuals reintegrate into society successfully.

To become a probation officer, candidates must undergo rigorous testing and training. Most jurisdictions require a bachelor's degree in criminal justice, social work, or psychology, and passing physical and psychological evaluations. This training equips them with the skills to handle the complexities of their job, including conflict resolution, crisis management, and effective communication. A good PO maintains their humanity and does not allow for ego to enter the conversation. They must be ethical, direct, and honest, embodying the qualities of a counselor while also being prepared to enforce the law.

A probation officer embodies both enforcement and support. This dual responsibility means monitoring compliance and offering guidance, all while prioritizing rehabilitation. The essence of their work is striking this ethical balance.

Personality traits common in law enforcement, such as assertiveness, pragmatism, and some skepticism, are essential for a probation officer. They must be ready to confront challenges head-on while maintaining empathy for those they supervise. This can sometimes create a perception of authoritarianism, where the officer's role seems oppressive rather than supportive.

However, while some POs may show authoritarian tendencies, many are genuinely invested in their clients' well-being.

Despite their authority, probation officers are not adversaries. Many individuals on probation may view their POs with suspicion or fear, feeling watched or judged. This perception can lead to a defensive attitude, where the probationer feels the need to hide or manipulate their behavior. If you focus on avoiding your probation officer and continue illegal activities and manipulation, you will not accept the help you need and will keep fighting the system, which will eventually lead to incarceration.

A probation officer is not a punisher but a facilitator. Their primary goal is protecting the public through rehabilitation. They are not responsible for your actions; rather, they are there to help you face the challenges of probation. The officer will watch over the probationer and hold them accountable with consequences they feel appropriate, but ultimate compliance is the responsibility of the probationer.

Probation officers are not infallible. They are human beings with their own vulnerabilities and challenges. Law enforcement personnel are vulnerable in many ways and often do not want others to know this. The stress of the job can affect their mental health, leading to issues such as PTSD, anxiety, and depression. Many officers see it as weakness to admit trauma or stress, let alone seek treatment. This reality highlights that probation officers are not just enforcers of the law; they are individuals who face significant challenges in their roles.

To foster a successful relationship between probation officers and their clients, mutual respect is essential. The two parties often come from different backgrounds and experiences, which can create tension. If both sides approach the relationship with an open mind, it can lead to positive outcomes. Differences in personalities may subside over time, allowing progress in the officer-client relationship. If not, and they maintain a level of discord, it will harm the probationer, not the officer.

A good probation officer will strive to build a trusting relationship with their clients, encouraging open communication and collaboration. They are not there to judge but to support and guide individuals toward a better path. If you've been given a good PO, they will have the following qualities: good listener, will hold you accountable, ethical, a willingness to help people, direct, and honest.

In conclusion, understanding the role of a probation officer requires recognizing their dual role as essential players in the criminal justice system, tasked with both enforcing the law and facilitating rehabilitation. While they may be seen as authoritarian figures, many are genuinely invested in the well-being of their clients. By fostering mutual respect and open communication, both probation officers and their clients can work together toward successful outcomes. Ultimately, the goal is not just compliance with the law but the successful reintegration of individuals into society, benefiting the individual and the community.

CHAPTER 6

ISOLATION IS BEST (FOR SOME)

Isolation is often considered the most effective approach for many individuals on probation, primarily because it can protect them from influences that might lead to re-offending. However, while isolation can offer protection and clarity, it may also cause significant harm to mental health and overall well-being.

For those on probation, isolation can feel paradoxical: it protects against negative influences but can also lead to feelings of loneliness and despair. Avoiding new relationships can help sidestep the stigma of probation, as revealing one's status may evoke shame. The rationale behind this is simple yet profound: one of the first questions that will likely arise in such relationships is: "Hey, you're not on probation, are you?"

A probation officer has a tough job. They make sure the rules of probation are followed, which might feel harsh. But it is important to see that their intentions are often rooted in a desire to help. The strict demands and harsh accountabilities they impose are not meant to hurt but to guide individuals toward a better life. Still, these rules can make probationers see officers as distant ally. This perception can further entrench the desire for isolation, as individuals may think they are always being watched.

While isolation can be perceived as a form of protection, it can also significantly change mental health. The act of withdrawing from social circles can create a fortress around oneself, keeping everyone out. Withdrawing may feel protective, but it can also lead to depression and anxiety. This is because the absence of social interaction can lead to a lack of emotional support, making it difficult to process the challenges of probation. If you notice negative feelings, seek support—professional help or trusted individuals can assist you in managing challenges. Relying only on isolation may make problems worse. Reaching out, even to a small support network, can provide important help while on probation.

Isolation frequently becomes a default survival strategy for those on probation, driven by the belief that old connections are risky. While this approach may protect against negative influences, the broader effect is a distorted sense of interpersonal relationships. A sharper view of isolation reveals it as both a shield against relapse and a risk to mental health—making it necessary to weigh its costs and benefits rather than accept it as the best solution for everyone.

During this period of isolation, use the opportunity to reflect on your life and growth. Visualizing life as the branches of a tree can be a helpful metaphor. Each branch represents different relationships, while the leaves symbolize various life events.

Some leaves may represent past mistakes and regrets, while other leaves symbolize positive experiences. Like trees shedding leaves in fall, probation is a chance to let go of what no longer serves you. Enduring the hardships of probation can lead to new beginnings in the spring, where growth and renewal are possible.

Remember, isolation does not require total withdrawal. For those in mandated group programs with other offenders, be cautious. While these sessions can offer valuable insights and support, close connections with other participants can be risky. Confiding in fellow offenders might lead to probation violations, jeopardizing the progress made during the probation period. It is essential to prioritize boundaries and personal safety as part of your overall strategy for a positive future.

The discipline gained through isolation can be empowering and help you say "no" when needed. However, this newfound discipline should not come at the cost of mental health. Find balance between protection from negative influences and maintaining well-being. Pursue solitary activities like reading or hobbies to constructively channel your thoughts, as these support your growth during probation.

Isolation is a double-edged sword. For some, it is a necessary strategy to navigate the complexities of probation successfully. For others, it can lead to feelings of loneliness and despair that are detrimental to mental health. It is essential to recognize that while isolation may provide a temporary sense of safety, it is not a one-size-fits-all solution. Each individual must assess their unique circumstances and determine the most constructive approach.

In conclusion, while isolation may be the most beneficial strategy for many probationers, it is crucial to remain vigilant about its potential pitfalls. The journey through probation is not merely about compliance; it is also an opportunity for growth, reflection, and transformation. By understanding the complexities of isolation and its impact on mental health, individuals can navigate their probationary period with greater awareness and intention. Whether through isolation or connection, the ultimate goal remains the same: to emerge from probation as a stronger, more resilient individual.

CHAPTER 7

YOU ARE NOT SAFE

While on probation, your personal safety is especially important. Focusing on putting yourself in safe situations should be a top priority. Most people think your vulnerability starts once a judge says, "Probation," but it often begins earlier, from the day of the incident. The terms and conditions of your probation are, believe it or not, your safety net. Probation often follows a situation that may have been unsafe—whether related to a confrontation, substance use, or harming another individual. Law enforcement personnel aim to keep everyone in the community safe, and that includes you. In some cases, if someone becomes a potential threat to the community, they may need to be temporarily separated for everyone's protection, including their own.

One of the most significant aspects of probation is adapting to restrictions placed for your protection. For example, you may be asked not to spend time with people from your past situations or with others who are currently on probation. This is designed to give you space from past influences and support better decision-making. You are not safe if the same people who influenced your past decisions are still in your life. This is common sense; it's a straightforward equation—one plus one equals two.

Consider this scenario: you are riding in your friend's vehicle, and he is driving recklessly. A cop pulls the car over and discovers a dead body in the trunk. You knew nothing about the dead body, but you're on probation, so you're automatically suspect number 1. If your probation includes restrictions on certain associations, following them is important. Yes, it usually is a condition of everyone's probation. You are not safe, and it is not smart to trust others with your freedom, even if it's your childhood best friend. This is a huge and common violation committed by many probationers, one that can greatly intensify your already strict requirements. Friends are an important part of life, but protecting your well-being and freedom must come first. Recognizing the importance of setting these boundaries helps ensure probation success and avoid further difficulties.

Your safety depends on your actions and how seriously you follow the terms of probation. Success or failure is mostly in your hands. Abide by your requirements, and you should be off probation within the mandated period. Failing to comply can lead to severe consequences, including incarceration.

To show why staying safe during probation matters, consider the statistics. The United States Bureau of Justice Statistics show that 57 percent of probationers complete probation successfully. The remaining 43 percent violate their probation, and 18 percent are incarcerated. These numbers are sad but realistic. Probation is hard by design. Its purpose is to discourage crime and encourage legal behavior. For some, not obeying the law can become an addictive cycle. Committing a crime or taking risks can provide an adrenaline rush. It may make you feel alive, but it can also take away your freedom. Stay safe and obey the terms and conditions of your probation.

Using, dealing, or transporting drugs will get you removed from your current housing. You may be placed somewhere stricter and more supervised. Drugs are a no-brainer; if you get caught with them, you're going somewhere uncomfortable. In the traditional scenario, the more times you are busted for drugs, the stricter your housing becomes. This cycle can lead to a downward spiral, where each violation compounds the consequences, making it increasingly difficult to recover and move forward.

According to the Bureau of Justice Statistics, at the end of 2020, an estimated 3,890,400 adults were on probation or parole. This is down 276,500 from January 1, 2020. These numbers show that about 1 in every 66 adults was on probation at the end of 2020. Many people navigate the complexities of probation, often without enough support or understanding of the risks involved.

The psychological toll of being on probation cannot be overlooked. Constant pressure to comply can lead to anxiety and stress. The fear of violating probation creates a heightened sense of vulnerability. This makes individuals feel as though they are walking on eggshells. This mental strain can lead to poor decision-making, putting safety and freedom at risk.

Moreover, the stigma associated with probation can isolate individuals from support networks. Friends and family may not understand the challenges, creating feelings of loneliness and despair. This isolation can push individuals back into situations that led to their initial offenses, continuing the cycle of criminal behavior.

To mitigate these risks, probationers must build a strong support system. Positive influences help with the challenges of probation. Using community resources, like counseling services, support groups, and rehabilitation programs, can provide the necessary tools to succeed.

Maintain open communication with your probation officer to create a sense of accountability. Hiding mistakes may be tempting, but honesty can lead to supportive interventions, not punitive measures. Probation officers want you to succeed. Show commitment to compliance and growth, and they may help more readily.

In conclusion, probation is filled with risks and challenges. Your vulnerability began long before the judge pronounced your sentence; it started with the choices that led to your offense. The terms and conditions of probation serve as a safety net. Upholding them takes diligence and commitment.

Stay away from negative influences. Adhere to the conditions of your probation, and seek support. These are essential steps in ensuring your safety while on probation. The statistics surrounding probation violations and incarceration rates highlight the reality that many individuals struggle to navigate this complex system. However, by taking personal responsibility and actively working toward compliance, you improve your chances of successfully completing probation and moving forward with your life.

Ultimately, your safety on probation is in your hands. Know the risks and make smart choices to avoid common pitfalls. Your freedom is worth protecting, and understanding the importance of your actions is the first step toward a better future.

CHAPTER 8

YOU ARE YOUR BIGGEST RAT

Probation can feel like a double-edged sword. It gives you a second chance to prove yourself, but it can also tighten around you if you're careless. In this precarious balance, the greatest threat often comes from within—yourself. The truth is, when you're on probation, you can easily become your own biggest rat.

Everyone knows the guy who ratted out his friends for a plea deal—the guy who walked away with no fair consequence. Everyone hates him; no one wants to be known as him. The sentiment is palpable: the "rat" carries a stigma that can follow someone for life. Players except for the rat may have received probation or worse, while it seems the dirty rat got away with it. However, when you find yourself in the grips of probation, it's crucial to remember you can betray yourself just as easily.

Once on probation, the biggest rat will be the reflection looking back at you in the mirror. That's right. Believe it or not, it's easy to become the rat in your own life when on probation. Self-sabotage often goes unnoticed until it's too late. You may think you're making good choices, but without vigilance, you can slip into old habits and be surrounded by the same crowd that led you astray in the first place.

One of the most glaring signs of a potential violation is the company you keep. Jim Rohn said it well, "You are the average of the 5 people you spend the most time with." If you're hanging out with the same crowd you were before probation, you're likely to repeat old behaviors. Changing or avoiding friends signals that you are trying to change. Associating with other probationers you've already been warned about is a violation that could send you back to court or jail.

Being seen with criminals exposes you. If your probation officer sees you with known offenders, it raises red flags and can jeopardize your probation status. Surrounding yourself with people who don't respect the law could easily draw you back into a lifestyle that you should be leaving behind.

Another big way you can get yourself in trouble is your phone. Your phone is not your private property while on probation; it is used to keep an eye on you. Your probation officer has access to everything on it. Photographs, texts, voicemails, contact lists, locations, and internet history all become hunting grounds for your PO.

Any mention of drugs, alcohol, weapons, or people you've been told not to contact can be grounds for a violation. Even seemingly innocent conversations can raise eyebrows. Think of your phone as an open book; anything on it can be scrutinized.

It's astonishing how easy it is to slip up by sending a text that you think is harmless but can lead to severe consequences.

Today, social media is another trap people can get caught off guard. Everyone on probation has to give their social media accounts to their PO. This is another layer of scrutiny, and it's a dangerous one. Imagine being tagged in a post by a known criminal or being seen at an event that violates your probation terms. Even if you don't engage, just being tagged could lead to a tough talk at your next meeting.

Staying off social media is not just a good idea; it's necessary. The vulnerability you expose yourself to is immense. Friends who don't understand your situation might tag you in posts or photos that complicate your standing with your probation officer. It's easy to underestimate how others can inadvertently put you at risk.

When you are on probation, you have to accept that your life is being watched. One way this plays out is through home searches. Probation officers can show up at your home without warning, armed with determination and latex gloves, searching for any sign of violations: alcohol, drugs, weapons, or even explicit material.

For people who take their probation lightly, these home searches can seem like a game, but for those who are serious about compliance, it's a nerve-wracking experience. Your car, your yard, your backpack, and even you can be searched at any time.

What happens if you're not home when your PO decides to pay a visit? It can lead to an automatic write-up. You may also end up with an ankle monitor that tracks your every move.

Modern ankle monitors can listen in on conversations and pinpoint your location. This gives your probation officer access to your life in a way that feels invasive.

In navigating probation, how you communicate is just as important as your actions. Certain phrases can be red flags for your probation officer. For example, saying "I should be clean" or "I'm not going to make probation" could signal a lack of confidence in your ability to adhere to the rules. Meanwhile, statements like "My friends are my life" can imply that you're not willing to avoid influences that led to your troubles.

If you say, "I just couldn't say no," it suggests a lack of personal responsibility. This is a significant concern for any probation officer. These phrases reveal an attitude that can put you on thin ice. So think carefully about how you express yourself.

Being your biggest rat is an easy problem to resolve. Just don't do anything wrong. It sounds simple, yet the reality is that staying on the straight and narrow requires vigilance and commitment. Surround yourself with positive influences, keep your digital footprint clean, and remember that your life is under a microscope.

Taking control of your choices and actions means being proactive. Seek out new friendships that uplift you and encourage you to be better. Set boundaries with old acquaintances who could lead you astray. The goal is to establish a support network that respects your commitment to change.

Probation is an opportunity for redemption, but it comes with challenges. If you're not careful, the biggest rat in your life can become your own reflection. Your choices, friends, and digital footprint can all contribute to your downfall. By understanding the pitfalls and working to avoid them, you can navigate probation and emerge stronger and more responsible. To avoid becoming your own rat, commit wholeheartedly to your transformation. The journey may be tough, but the reward of freedom and a fresh start is worth the effort.

CHAPTER 9

DRUGS = LOCK UP, EVENTUALLY

When you're on probation, the stakes are high. Every decision you make has the potential to either move you toward a stable future or lead you straight back to a cell. Choosing to engage in drug use while on probation significantly increases your likelihood of serving time. To be clear: consistent drug use while under supervision puts you at serious risk of incarceration.

Engaging in drug use while on probation is a direct and blatant violation of your release terms. Failing a drug test (often called "popping hot" on a urinalysis) is a clear-cut violation—one of the easiest for a court to prove. Probation officers are trained to look for these signs, and failing a drug test sends a direct message that you're still struggling with addiction.

If your drug levels are rising after being placed on probation, you are effectively demonstrating an inability to remain safe within the community. The core purpose of probation is to allow you to reintegrate into society while adhering to specific conditions. When you choose to ingest drugs, it becomes evident that you're not ready for that responsibility. Your PO will then be compelled to fulfill their duty, which may involve revoking your probation and incarcerating you for your own safety and that of the community.

Addiction is a pervasive issue that has plagued humanity for ages. It chemically manipulates the brain, causing things you once cared about to become mere shadows. Family, work, and future aspirations often dissolve into insignificance as the pursuit of the next fix becomes all that matters. If your first thought upon waking is how to obtain drugs, you have a serious problem.

It's important to understand that initial drug experimentation is a choice, but staying on drugs until your life is destroyed is often a disease. Addiction doesn't discriminate; it can ensnare anyone, transforming them into an unrecognizable version of themselves. When your life revolves around substance use, the consequences are dire—not only for you but also for everyone around you.

If you find yourself struggling with addiction while on probation, it's crucial to inform your probation officer. Yes, help can come in the form of community-based programs or residential treatment. While this sometimes involves placement in a criminal justice facility, the ultimate goal remains the same: cessation of drug use. Unfortunately, for some individuals, achieving lasting success in this process may require multiple attempts.

Relapses are a common part of the recovery journey, but they are particularly perilous while on probation. If you relapse and your PO finds out, you could face severe penalties, including incarceration. The message is clear: if you use drugs, you jeopardize your freedom and severely worsens your overall legal situation.

It's vital to understand that all substances carry the risk of addiction, including marijuana. While addiction manifests differently for everyone, the psychological dependency can be just as potent as physical addiction. Humans possess both strengths and vulnerabilities. Overcoming the weakness of addiction requires immense personal strength, but achieving that victory makes life more manageable.

Clients who use drugs while on probation are often automatically assumed to be addicts. After all, why would someone consciously risk prison time if they were not chemically dependent? Those who actively use often go through a dark cycle: some may need to experience incarceration before they realize the need to get clean. Others may require a hospital visit due to an overdose. Tragically, some may even face the grave consequence of death before they can truly confront their addiction.

Probation officers navigate a challenging landscape filled with individuals grappling with addiction. Their primary goal is to help, but this requires a complex balancing act of accountability and support. They understand that for many of their clients, the drug they perceive as their best friend is, in reality, their most significant enemy.

When traditional methods of support fail, incarceration emerges as the final tool to interrupt the cycle of addiction. While it may seem counterintuitive, time behind bars can provide a much-needed reprieve from the chaos of addiction. It offers 24-7 supervision and an environment where individuals can begin to heal. For some, this enforced sobriety is the catalyst they need to see how addiction is eroding their life, happiness, and freedom.

Addiction is a beast with sharp, jagged teeth, capable of inflicting profound emotional and physical damage. The human cost is staggering. Individuals lose their families, their jobs, and sometimes their lives. They become shells of their former selves, numb to the world around them.

Probation cannot cure addiction, but it can be a starting point for recovery. Skills learned during probation, such as accountability, self-discipline, and coping mechanisms, can be pivotal for long-term recovery. However, success rates are unfortunately low. Many probation officers handle a caseload filled with addicts, which can skew their overall success metrics.

Dealing with drug addiction is one of the most complicated challenges for both probationers and officers. Addicts are often at higher risk of reoffending, driven by the need for drugs. This cycle can create a ripple effect, leading to theft and exploitation of vulnerable people, including family members and the elderly. These defenseless individuals may find themselves victimized by those they love, which complicates recovery for everyone involved.

The best-case scenario for families dealing with an active addict on probation is to seek help from the probation officer. It's a difficult and heartbreaking situation, but POs are well-equipped to handle it. They are trained to intervene and provide support, not just to hold the individual accountable.

If you use drugs while on probation, you are your own victim. The choices you make dictate your future. Your probation officer is there to help, but they cannot let you continue on a path that leads to self-destruction. If you keep using drugs, you jeopardize your freedom and hurt yourself and everyone around you.

In probation, the consequences of drug use are serious and often life-altering. Substance use can lead to incarceration, which is not just a physical lockup but a prison of the mind and spirit. To break free from this cycle, you must confront the addiction and take proactive steps toward recovery. Your future, happiness, and freedom depend on it. The road may be difficult, but choosing sobriety is the first step toward reclaiming your life.

CHAPTER 10

PROBATION LIFE-ER

In most circumstances, probation does not last indefinitely. This is a fundamental truth that everyone under supervision must accept. While probation can feel like an endless sentence filled with restrictions and anxiety, it is a temporary phase designed to guide individuals toward a better path. The reality is that if offenders continue to violate terms and commit more crimes, they will eventually "level up" to prison and may later find themselves on parole rather than probation.

One of the more perplexing behaviors observed in those nearing the end of their probation is self-sabotage. Some individuals start to believe that complete freedom will grant them too much opportunity for failure, worrying that their old habits will resurface without the stringent guidance of a probation officer (PO). This mentality can lead to reckless decisions and outright violations, often rooted in the misconception that they will remain under the watchful eye of their PO indefinitely. Instead of finding freedom, they often find themselves incarcerated, which is a harsh awakening to the consequences of their actions.

Some people thrive on chaos, feeling more alive when surrounded by drama. For them, probation might even serve as a safety net—a structured environment where they feel protected from their own destructive behaviors. It's a paradoxical situation: while probation is intended to encourage compliance and rehabilitation, it can also become a comfortable, self-imposed prison for those who fear the responsibilities of complete freedom.

When the time comes for probation to expire, the process is not as simple as it might seem. The probation officer is required to answer very specific questions about the probationer. These answers establish details regarding compliance or lack thereof. They must document any violations or arrests, and there's usually an entire team involved in making the final determination regarding the probationer's readiness to move past supervision.

This team often includes the PO, the district attorney, and sometimes a judge. If any party wishes to extend the probation period due to non-compliance, they can take the matter back to court. It's a collective decision, underscoring the importance of maintaining good standing while under supervision.

Probation is inherently temporary. While some individuals may face just a few months of supervision, others might be mandated to remain on probation for five years or more. Regardless of the duration, the key point is that this period is not meant to last forever. It serves as a critical time of monitoring, offering individuals the chance to demonstrate their ability to live within the law.

The choices you make during probation are crucial. You already know what it takes to live a healthy life and keep yourself out of trouble. As your probation nears its end, the responsibility shifts fully back into your own hands. This transition can be one of the most frightening aspects of probation—the prospect of being completely unsupervised can be overwhelming.

There is a possibility for early termination of probation, but this is not easily granted. You may need to enlist the help of an attorney to file the necessary paperwork, or sometimes, your PO can handle this for you once you express the desire for early release. However, without the PO's consent, an early termination is highly unlikely.

To be considered for early termination, the probationer must be in good standing—meaning they have completed all court mandates, paid fines, and demonstrated a clear commitment to staying crime-free. In short, the path to an early exit from probation hinges heavily on the relationship between the probationer and their officer.

While on probation, many individuals experience a heightened level of paranoia, often likened to being a zebra in a lion-infested den. They become hyper-aware of their surroundings, constantly trying to avoid unwanted encounters with their probation officer. The looming fear of being reported by someone from their past can create a persistent atmosphere of anxiety and distress.

After enduring this stress for years, regaining a sense of normalcy once probation ends can take several months. This experience can resemble a form of post-traumatic stress disorder (PTSD), where the individual struggles to adjust to a life free from constant surveillance. Though it brings immense relief, this transition demands a significant recalibration of one's entire mindset.

Despite the obvious challenges, probation can lead to significant personal growth and change. If you follow the rules and complete all requirements, you will likely find that your life has improved dramatically. The skills learned during this period—especially accountability and self-discipline—become invaluable. Once supervision is terminated, you can reflect on the distance you've traveled and the healthier lifestyle you've successfully adopted.

Moreover, one of the most critical outcomes of completing probation is the ability to secure stable employment without the stress associated with illegal activities. You can find a job that offers legal income, providing both financial stability and genuine peace of mind. This newfound freedom can be exhilarating and empowering.

Completing probation brings a profound sense of closure. The nagging paranoia of knowing your PO can show up at any moment becomes a thing of the past. You can genuinely relax, free from the fear that a missed call or an unexpected sound outside your home could lead to an arrest or violation.

The mental liberation from this constant state of alertness is transformative. The lingering fears associated with supervision often fade with time, allowing individuals to embrace life more fully. While adjustment requires patience, the clarity that emerges once the dust settles is a powerful, life-altering reward.

Probation is undoubtedly tough, but remember that this journey is temporary. It serves as a vital steppingstone toward personal accountability and a better life. Once you complete your supervision, you'll find yourself equipped with the tools necessary to navigate the world without the weight of your past actions holding you back.

Ultimately, your experiences during probation can lead to a healthier, more fulfilling life—if you allow them to. Remember, you cannot be on probation forever. The end of this chapter is not just a release from supervision; it's an opportunity to reclaim your life and chart a new course. Make the most of it. The choices you make moving forward will determine your future, and with each positive decision, you pave the way for a life unencumbered by the past.

CONCLUSION

In closing, navigating the complexities of probation is no small feat. It's disheartening when you try repeatedly to make changes in your life, only to find yourself back in the same troubled situation. This cycle is often self-sabotage, but recognizing these destructive patterns is the critical first step toward breaking free.

Self-sabotage manifests in various ways: blaming others, deflecting responsibility, and playing the victim. It can also involve quitting a task because you think it's too hard to follow through, leading to a frustrating cycle of defeat. Often, procrastination creeps in when you lack confidence, effectively robbing you of the motivation and discipline needed to achieve your goals.

Other self-destructive behaviors include being overly sensitive and taking things too seriously, which can lead to unnecessary arguments. Conversely, failing to stand up for your own needs only perpetuates a feeling of powerlessness. Insulting yourself or doubting your worth creates an internal environment where genuine change feels impossible.

Moreover, the fear associated with being on probation can itself trigger bouts of self-sabotage, causing you to act directly against your own best interests. It's crucial to understand that while self-sabotage may feel like a temporary way out, it ultimately leads to consequences that could escalate substantially—perhaps even resulting in further legal troubles.

Don't hold yourself back by engaging in these behaviors. Instead, embrace the tools and insights you've gained. Remember that change is possible, and it begins with you taking full responsibility for your actions. By being mindful of these self-destructive patterns and committing to a path of personal growth, you can create a future that extends far beyond probation.

As you move forward, keep in mind that the journey is yours to shape. Empower yourself to make choices that truly reflect your desires and goals. The lessons learned during probation can serve as a powerful foundation for a fulfilling life. You have the strength to overcome the obstacles in your path—don't let self-sabotage dim your potential. Your future awaits; it's time to step into it with confidence and purpose.

www.ingramcontent.com/pod-product-compliance
Lightning Source LLC
LaVergne TN
LVHW101617210926
848480LV00009B/794
* 9 7 9 8 8 9 2 2 8 7 9 1 3 *